IT'S UP TO YOU...

What Do You Do?

IT'S UP TO YOU...
What Do You Do?

Sandra McLeod Humphrey

Illustrated by Brian Strassburg

 **Prometheus Books**

59 John Glenn Drive
Amherst, New York 14228-2197

Published 1999 by Prometheus Books

03 02 01 00 99   5 4 3 2 1

Interior design by Jacqueline Cooke
Illustrated by Brian Strassburg

Library of Congress Cataloging-in-Publication Data

Humphrey, Sandra McLeod.
    It's up to you . . . what do you do? / Sandra McLeod Humphrey ; illustrated by
Brian Strassburg.
    p.   cm.
    Summary: A collection of short stories, with "thought questions," each illustrating
a lesson about such moral principles as kindness, forgiveness, respect, honesty, and
good sportsmanship.
    ISBN 1-57392-263-3 (alk. paper)
    [1. Conduct of life—Fiction. 2. Parables.] I. Strassburg, Brian, ill. II. Title.
PZ8.2.H78It   1999
[Fic]—dc21   98-47664
                                                                                          CIP
                                                                                          AC

Printed in the United States of America on acid-free paper

Dedicated to young people everywhere
and to those who care about them.

Contents

A Note to Adults

Webster's Dictionary defines a parable as "a short fictitious story that illustrates a moral attitude or a religious principle."

The twenty-five parables in this book illustrate various principles that serve to define strong character such as personal integrity, compassion, loyalty, perseverance, self-discipline, and personal accountability as well as many others.

By reading these stories with your children or students and discussing the thought questions at the end of each story, you will have the opportunity to share your ideas about why such principles are so important. You may even want to talk about people you may know who demonstrate these principles.

A Note to the Young Reader

The twenty-five stories in this book are about people who have to make tough decisions based on moral principles. Moral principles are things such as kindness, compassion, honesty, respect for others, and good sportsmanship. You can probably think of many others.

Read these stories with your parents or in your classroom at school and share your ideas with your classmates, friends, family, and others. The questions at the end of each story will help you get started thinking about some of the interesting problems in each story. Sharing your ideas with others can help you decide which principles or values are really important to you and help you become the person you want to be.

Now the most important point I want to make: Have fun with this book! Talk over the stories with different people when you feel like it and sometimes just read them when you are by yourself. Whether alone or with others, enjoy this book the same way you would enjoy a good friend.

It's Up to You . . .
What Do You Do?

B-O-R-I-N-G!

Keri and Allison stared at their homework assignment. No one should be expected to read a book that long in less than a week—and write a book report.

Keri thumbed through the book to the last page. "Look at this, almost one hundred pages! It'll take me forever to get through this."

Allison smiled and shook her head. "No, it won't. My mom's got the audiocassette for this book at home. All we have to do is listen to the cassette and then write the book report. We can even play video games while we listen to the cassette. No sweat."

Keri closed the book and nodded. "Okay, bring the cassette over tomorrow after school and we can listen to it then."

The next day in school, Ms. Murphy showed the class a film about Thomas Edison, Abraham Lincoln, Albert Einstein, Eleanor Roosevelt, and Arthur Ashe. Then she asked the class, "What did all these people have in common?"

The class just looked blank and both Keri and Allison shook their heads. They didn't have any idea what these people had in common.

Ms. Murphy moved to the front of the class and sat on the corner of her desk. "Okay, I'll give you a clue. What did all these people do?"

The class still looked confused, but Keri raised her hand and volunteered.

"Thomas Edison was a famous inventor, Lincoln was a famous president, and Einstein was a famous scientist. Mrs. Roosevelt was the wife of a president and did a lot of things to help other people—kind of like Princess Diana—and Arthur Ashe was a famous tennis player. They were all famous people, but I don't think they were very much alike at all."

Allison was the next to raise her hand. "I agree with Keri. I don't think they were alike either. Some were men and one was a woman and they all had different jobs. So what did they have in common?"

Ms. Murphy smiled. "Think about the film. Did all of these people have a lot of problems? And did any of these people give up or take the easy way out when they had a problem?"

William was the next to volunteer. "Yes, to the first question and no to the second. All those guys had big problems. Edison failed thousands of times before he got his inventions to work, and Lincoln lost more elections than he won before he was finally elected president."

Then Allison's hand shot back up. "And how about Mrs. Roosevelt? One of her aunts told her she was the 'ugly duckling' of the family, but she just kept on doing her own thing and helping people anyway. And Arthur Ashe faced a lot of racial discrimination in his tennis tournaments, but he just kept on going, too. They all just kept on going like the Energizer bunny until they succeeded at what they were trying to do. No one gave up."

Ms. Murphy smiled again and gave her a thumbs-up. "You got it. All of these people just kept going in spite of their problems. No one gave up or took the easy way out, and what did it get them?"

16

Keri raised her hand again. "That's easy. They all got to be so famous that we read about them in books. I guess hard work pays off in the end."

The bell rang and Ms. Murphy put the video back in its case. "Okay, class, just think about the film and we'll talk about it some more tomorrow."

After school, Allison came over to Keri's house. She had her mom's audiocassette for the book they both had to read and she told Keri she was ready to get started.

Allison grinned as she put the cassette in the tape player and turned it on. "This is going to be a piece of cake."

Keri turned the tape player off and said, "Wait a minute. Let's be sure we want to do this."

Do you think Keri is going to read the book or listen to the cassette? Why?

More to think about:

If you were Keri, what would you do? Why?

What do you think Allison will do?

What do you think Ms. Murphy would do if she found out the girls hadn't really read the book?

Do you think that some people might call listening to the cassette instead of reading the book a form of cheating? Why or why not?

When you have to do something that is really hard, do you think it's okay to take the easy way out? Why or why not?

To Bury or to Spend

Cindy, Ashley, and Betsy waved good-bye to their grandfather and watched as his airplane glided down the runway and took off.

His visit had been great as usual. They had gone to movies, fished for hours from the dock, and had picnic lunches almost every day. That morning as they helped him pack his bags, they wished that he never had to leave and could stay with them forever.

As their grandfather closed his last bag, he told them that he had something very special for them. Then he gave each sister an envelope with fifty dollars in it and told them they could use their money in any way they wanted. It was his special gift to each of them.

Although the girls were triplets and looked a lot alike, they didn't always think the same way about everything. They had all been taught the importance of saving money as well as the importance of spending money wisely, so they did a lot of serious thinking about what to do with their gifts. Then each one came up with a different plan.

Cindy wanted to be sure that nothing happened to her money, so she hid it in a corner of her closet under her shoe shelf, where she knew it would be safe and where no one else would be able to find it. Then when their grandfather visited them again at Christmas, she would show him the whole fifty dollars still safe and sound just as he had given it to her.

She didn't even write anything in her diary about where the money was hidden. She wasn't taking any chances that someone might find the money. She wanted to be sure that her money stayed right where it was until she saw Grandpa again.

Ashley thought a long time about her fifty dollars and then finally decided to put her money in a bank where it could earn some interest and increase in value over the next few months. She called all three neighborhood banks and found out that one bank had a special college account where her money would earn higher interest than if she just put her money in a regular savings account. That sounded good to her, so she decided that was where she would put her money. She would do what she heard Mom and Dad talk about. She would "invest" in her future.

Ashley could hardly wait until their grandfather returned at Christmas to show him how her money had grown in her account and yet she was able to keep it in a safe place where nothing could happen to it. She knew that no one could have done more with their fifty dollars than she had and she was feeling really great about her plan.

After a lot of thought, Betsy finally made her decision about what to do with her fifty dollars. Her class was taking donations to sponsor a young boy named Vinod in India. The money would be used to buy clothes and school supplies and medicine. Then each donation was going to be matched by a big computer company in their city.

That meant her money would really be worth one hundred dollars once it was matched by the computer company and she would also be helping her class reach their goal of supporting Vinod for an entire year.

Betsy felt pleased with her decision and was sure that when Grandpa returned at Christmas, he would also be pleased.

Which of the three sisters do you think put her money to its best use? Why?

More to think about:

Why do you think Cindy hid her money?

What do you think of Ashley's plan?

What do you think of Betsy's plan?

What do you think their grandfather will say when he finds out what each girl has done with her money?

What would you have done with the money? Why?

Down but Not Out

Ben Bronson could still hear Dan's cries of pain as he fell into the water from the high-diving board. It was almost a year since the accident, but every time Ben looked at his brother, it brought back memories of that terrible day.

He still remembered how scared he felt as he saw Dan go crashing into the water, his body twisting and turning like a rag doll. And he still remembered how afraid he had felt as he dove in after his brother, not knowing if Dan would be dead or alive.

Dan would have to stay in his wheelchair stuck with his disability for the rest of his life while Alex had gotten off scot-free. Alex was the "class clown," and if he hadn't been fooling around on the high-diving board, the accident would never have happened. If it hadn't been for Alex, Dan never would have slipped off the end of the board, and he would still be on the track team.

Instead, it was Alex who was on the school track team. It was Alex who was winning track medals every week. And it was Alex who still had the use of his legs while Dan would be stuck in a wheelchair. It just wasn't fair.

Ben didn't understand why Dan still went to the track meets and rooted for Alex. He didn't understand why Dan was always one of the first ones to congratulate Alex on his wins.

Ben couldn't even go to the track meets, and if he had gone, he certainly wouldn't be cheering for Alex.

It had taken months of rehabilitation, but now Dan was back in school and had almost caught up with the rest of his class, thanks to special tutors at the rehab center. Some of Dan's teachers had even dropped his work off at home for him, so that he could keep up with the rest of his class.

During the long months at the rehab center, Dan had plenty of time to think and he had done a lot of it. He had always been a good student and he decided that he might like to study to be an attorney like their dad.

Dan would never forget the accident. How could he? But he decided to make the best of a bad situation and get on with his life.

Ben, on the other hand, promised never to forgive Alex. Every time he looked at his brother in his wheelchair, he felt angry all over again. Ben began to spend less time with his friends and more time in his room by himself, thinking about ways he could even the score for his brother.

At first, their dad had been more concerned about Dan. After the accident he didn't want to talk to anyone. He seemed to be mad at the whole world and everyone in it. He went to his physical therapy sessions at the rehab center but refused to go out or to talk to anyone.

Then Dan started feeling really bad about himself. The doctor called it being depressed. Dan still wasn't talking to anyone, and his family and friends were very worried about him. Finally Dan's doctor persuaded him to begin attending group talk sessions even if he didn't feel like saying anything.

Slowly Dan seemed to pull himself together and began to talk about his plans for the future. He began to hit the books hard and the last two weeks he had even started going to the track meets again.

Now Mr. Bronson was more concerned about Ben who seemed to be spending more and more time by himself, just locked up in his room listening to his music.

Ben had dropped out of the basketball team and was no longer even playing his guitar.

Which brother do you think has the greater disability? Why?

More to think about:

Do you think Dan has forgiven Alex?

Why do you think Ben is still so angry?

How do you think Alex feels?

What do you think will happen to Dan?

What do you think will happen to Ben?

A Dream Come True

Willie always got whatever he wanted. His dad owned his own plumbing business and there was always plenty of money for whatever Willie wanted or needed. Whatever Willie wanted, Willie got.

And this birthday was no exception. Willie got the bike of his dreams—a ten-speed racing bike with all the latest high-tech equipment. Even the color was perfect. Red, his favorite color. Willie was feeling on top of the world and could hardly wait to show his new bike to his best friend, Jason.

Jason's dad had been out of work for the last six months, so times were rough for everyone in Jason's family. Jason had found a job delivering newspapers every morning before school to earn money for a new bike since he knew there was no way his family could afford to buy him one. He had also started taking his lunch to school every day to save even more money for his bike.

Jason had been saving for over three months now and had managed to save enough to begin seriously looking for a bike. And he knew just what it would look like. It would be a flashy fire-engine-red ten-speed with a racing seat and all the neat stuff his friends had on their bikes. After he got his brand-new bike, he would give his old one to his kid brother, Curtis. His old bike would be just the right size for his brother.

On his way home from school after track practice, Jason stopped at a neighbor's garage sale to see if there was anything worth buying since his brother's birthday was coming up in another month.

Jason found some used games for only two dollars and an old chess set for one dollar and decided those would make great birthday gifts for his brother. He was about to pay for the games and the chess set when he spotted a used bike in the corner of the garage.

The bike was pretty scratched up and it didn't look much like the classy ten-speed he had been dreaming about, but the price was right. He had enough money in his savings bank at home to pay for the bike and it would be great to finally have a bike his size instead of having to ride the old one he had outgrown two years ago.

Green was not his favorite color, but Jason figured he could repaint the bike any color he wanted and he knew his dad would be glad to help him fix it up.

Jason paid for the games and the chess set and then asked the neighbor to hold the bike for him while he went home to get the rest of his money.

All the way home, Jason kept thinking about all the ways he could fix up his new bike until it would look even better than new. A new paint job would be just the beginning. Then a new seat, a new headlight, and maybe a holder for his water bottle.

The more he thought about all the things he could do with his new bike, the more excited he got. He wouldn't be able to do everything at once, but by the time he was finished with it, it would be one super bike. It would be almost like making the bike all over again from scratch because everything would be done just the way he wanted it. Nobody else would have a bike just like his.

By the time Jason got back to the garage sale with his money, he was feeling on top of the world and could hardly wait to show his new bike to his best friend, Willie.

Which boy do you think will appreciate his new bike more? Why?

More to think about:

What will Willie think of Jason's bike?

What will Jason think of Willie's bike?

Who do you think will take better care of his bike? Why?

How do you feel when you earn something yourself?

Have you ever wanted something as much as these boys wanted their bikes?

Easy Come, Easy Go

Julie was on her way out the front door when her mother reminded her not to forget her money for the Santa Anonymous program at school.

This year her class had decided to contribute money to the Santa Anonymous fund to buy Christmas presents for kids whose families couldn't afford to buy gifts. Today was the day to turn the money in and Julie could still hear the principal's last words. "Remember, for some of these kids, Christmas is just another day without enough food or any warm clothes. So try to give something up to make a difference for one of these kids. Make a sacrifice, so that a kid can have a real Christmas."

Julie ran back upstairs to get her money, but she found her Garfield bank bone dry. Then she remembered that she had spent the last of her allowance on a pizza when she had gone out with Lisa last Friday.

She had meant to put back the money, but then she had to buy new guitar strings, so there was nothing left to put in her bank.

Julie told her mother that she was broke again and so she wouldn't be able to contribute anything to the Santa Anonymous fund. Julie's mother told her not to worry about it and gave her a ten-dollar bill out of the kitchen cookie jar. Julie stuffed the bill into her backpack and then hurried off next door to pick up her best friend, Lisa.

Julie found Lisa upstairs in her bedroom. Her guitar bank was turned upside down on her bed and she was counting all her money.

Lisa grinned as Julie flopped down on the bed next to her. "Look, Julie, I've saved up twenty dollars already and I've only been saving for two weeks.

"Most of it is from my birthday last week. Ten is a gift from my grand-father, five is from my brother because he couldn't think of anything to buy me, and five is what I already had saved from my allowance."

Julie picked up the bank and emptied out the last two pennies. "So are you giving the whole twenty to the Santa Anonymous fund?"

Lisa carefully separated her savings into two piles. "Are you crazy, girl? Ten goes to Santa Anonymous and ten goes for that awesome T-shirt we saw at the mall yesterday. Remember, the black one with the skeleton that shines in the dark?"

Julie stuffed the money for Lisa's T-shirt back into her bank while Lisa stuffed the money for Santa Anonymous into the side pocket of her back-pack. Then both girls hurried down the street to Megan's house where they found her waiting on the front porch for them.

Julie pulled her ten-dollar bill out of her backpack and showed it to Megan. "Look, Megan, I'm giving ten dollars to the Santa Anonymous fund at school and so is Lisa. How much are you giving?"

Megan unzipped the front pocket of her backpack and counted out ten one-dollar bills. "I'm giving ten dollars, too. These are the three dollars I earned for cleaning out the garage, these are the four dollars I earned babysitting the Nelson twins, and these are the three dollars I had stashed away in my Esmerelda bank."

As the girls stuffed their money back into their backpacks, Julie smiled. "Don't you think it's an awesome coincidence that we're all giving exactly the same gift to the Santa Anonymous fund? We didn't even talk about it and yet here we are all giving exactly the same thing."

The girls closed up their backpacks and headed off for school, each girl feeling good about her gift for Santa Anonymous.

Do you think each of the three girls really gave exactly the same gift to the Santa Anonymous fund? Why or why not?

More to think about:

What do you think about Julie's gift?

What about Lisa's gift?

And what about Megan's gift?

Which girl made the greatest sacrifice?

Which girl's gift do you think meant the most to her? Why?

If you were receiving food or clothing from the Santa Anonymous fund, whose gift would mean the most to you?

Get a Life

Ms. Murphy waited for the bell and then began. "Okay, class, listen up. Today, I'm going to tell you a little story about three brothers.

"All three brothers were looking for summer jobs, but the only job they could find was mopping floors in a large supermarket.

"The oldest brother, Tim, thought he should be doing a much more important job, so he spent most of his time just leaning on his mop dreaming about what he would be doing some day when he was president of his own company.

"He could see it all now. He would go to work every morning in a long white limo driven by a chauffeur in a gray uniform.

"His office would be on the very top floor of the tallest building and one of the windows in his office would cover the entire wall, so that he could sit at his desk and look down on the whole world below him.

"And he would make so much money that he would never be able to spend it all, so he would give some of it away to his two younger brothers, Gordon and Adam.

"While Tim was daydreaming about being president of his own company, the middle brother, Gordon, groaned and moaned as he pushed his mop up and down the aisles. He just knew that he would have a sore back and be stiff as a board if he mopped all the floors that were assigned to him, so he looked for ways to make his job easier.

"Gordon never moved any of the cardboard boxes stacked in the aisles. He just mopped around them. He was sure that no one would ever know that he hadn't moved them, so why break his back doing stuff he didn't have to do?

"And when the water in his bucket got dirty, he never emptied it and got fresh water. He just kept mopping the floor with the same dirty water. After all, who would ever know that he never changed the water?

"Gordon knew that some day he would be very rich. It was just a matter of finding the easiest way to do everything. And he knew that he was very good at that. He could always find the easiest way to do something without even trying.

"The youngest brother, Adam, didn't like mopping floors any more than his brothers did, but he believed that it was important to do your best on any job—whether it was a small job or a big job, whether the job was easy or hard.

"Both Tim and Gordon told Adam he was a real jerk to work so hard on stupid jobs that weren't even important, jobs that didn't count for anything.

"Whenever Tim saw Adam hard at work mopping his aisles, he slapped him hard on the back and said, 'Get a life, kid. You're never going to get anywhere wasting your time doing stupid stuff like this. You'll be mopping floors the rest of your life while Gordon and I are raking in the money and watching other guys mop floors for us.'

"And when Gordon saw Adam hard at work mopping, he said, 'If you keep working that hard, you're going to wear yourself out before you ever get a *real* job. Get a life, kid, a *real* life. There's more to life than mopping floors, but you're never going to make it big if you waste your time doing stupid stuff like this. You're still going to be mopping floors while Tim and I are driving around in our limos.'

"In spite of what his brothers said, Adam just kept right on mopping his floors and doing the best job he could. And sometimes he even helped his brothers mop their floors, so that they could all finish up at the same time and go home together."

Which brother do you think is going to be the most successful many years from now? Why?

More to think about:

How do you think Tim is handling his responsibilities?

How do you think Gordon is handling his responsibilities?

How do you think Adam is handling his responsibilities?

Which brother do you respect the most? Why?

Do you think there's such a thing as an "unimportant" job? Why or why not?

In Over His Head

Eric was drowning in math problems. He had always hated word problems and now he had ten of them and he didn't understand any of them. He needed help, and fast!

Eric found his older brother, Tom, watching TV in the den and right away Tom offered to help. Tom showed Eric that he didn't really have any problem at all because all the answers were in the back of the book. All Eric had to do was copy down the answers now and then figure out how to do the problems later when he didn't have so much to do. His brother explained that there was always an easy way out for every problem. All you had to do was look for it.

As Eric passed the kitchen, he saw his older sister, Angie, frosting a cake for dinner. Angie was a real whiz at math and she immediately offered to help him.

Angie whipped a sheet of paper out of her notebook and sat down at the kitchen table with Eric's math book. It took her less than twenty minutes to do the problems and then she handed the finished paper to Eric with a big smile.

She let him lick the frosting bowl and told him to come back any time he needed more help.

Eric was on his way back up to his room when he noticed his dad reading the newspaper in the living room. He asked Eric how he was coming with his math. Eric shrugged and told his dad that he didn't really understand it yet but that he was working on it.

His dad pulled out some paper and a pen from his briefcase and offered to help him with the first three problems. After they had worked out the first three problems, his dad told Eric to try to figure out the rest of the problems for himself and then they would go over them together when he was done.

Eric thanked his dad and headed back upstairs to his room where he found his mom stacking a pile of clean clothes on his bed. She asked him how his math was coming along.

He told her that he understood the first three problems now, but he wasn't so sure about the rest of them. She sat down on his bed and told him to show her the problems.

His mother read through the word problems and then marked down the page numbers in his math book where each different kind of word problem was explained. She handed the book back to Eric and told him to read the pages she had marked and then he would understand how to do all ten problems.

Eric sat down at his desk, but instead of opening his math book, he found himself thinking about his family. Everyone had been more than willing to help him.

His brother had shown him where to look up the answers, so he could hand his assignment in on time without having to sweat over the problems. That was definitely the easy way out all right. He could always study his math better later when he had more time.

His sister had done his whole assignment for him without blinking an eye. All he had to do was copy her answers onto his math sheet and he had it made.

His dad had helped him work out the first three problems, but after that, he was on his own. And it was like being back to square one. He still didn't have any idea how to do the last seven problems.

His mom had shown him which pages to study to understand the different word problems, but reading all those pages would take a lot of time. And why should he do that when he already had all the answers?

Everyone in Eric's family helped him in a different way. Who do you think helped him the most? Why?

More to think about:

How much did Tom really help Eric?

How much did Angie really help Eric?

How much did Eric's dad help him?

How much did Eric's mom help him?

If you were Eric, what would you do?

Inside Out

Travis waited impatiently while Coach Benson posted the names for the hockey team on the school bulletin board. Finally the crowd thinned out enough, so Travis could read the list himself.

The names were alphabetical, so he started at the end of the list. No Travis Winston! He began again, this time at the beginning. He read through every name on the list and then read every name again, just to be sure. But there was still no Travis Winston.

He felt really bad. Making the sixth-grade hockey team was the most important thing in his life. His best friend, Derek, had made the team and even Marcus, the new kid, had made the team.

He was shuffling back to his math class when he ran into Derek. Derek pounded him on the back and congratulated him. "Good going, guy. You got the lead role in the class play. You landed the part of the Beast and Shari got the part of Belle. Some guys have all the luck."

Suddenly Travis felt like a million bucks. He never dreamed he'd get the lead role in the class play, *Beauty and the Beast*. This was the first year he had ever tried out. Usually, he just ended up painting scenery and working the lights. Wow, this was really great!

Ms. Eaton was just handing out yesterday's social studies tests as Travis slipped into his seat. He unfolded his test and couldn't believe his eyes. But there it was, a huge red "D." He knew he hadn't studied for the test, but how could he have gotten a D? He had never ever gotten a D in any subject.

He was such a loser! How would he give his parents the bad news? He would probably lose all his TV privileges for a week and be stuck in his room studying stupid social studies every night for the rest of his life. Boy, this was one of the worst days of his whole life.

When the bell finally rang, he met Derek in the cafeteria for lunch. "Boy, guy, did you luck out! The *Metro Daily* is going to do a big news story on our class play, and you and Shari are going to get your pictures in the paper and everything. I'd give up my place on the hockey team just to be in your shoes right now."

Travis dug into his sandwich with a wide grin. Lunch had never tasted so good. Wow, an interview by a real reporter. And his picture in the paper with Shari. She was just about the most popular girl in the whole school. Maybe he should even think about starting a scrapbook.

By the time Travis got home from school, he could hardly wait to tell his parents the great news about the play, but no one was home. He found a note on the refrigerator door. His dad wouldn't be back from Chicago till the next day and his mom had taken his sister to the hospital and wouldn't be home till late. There was meat loaf in the fridge and could he please fold the clothes in the dryer?

Bummer! Here he was all ready to tell everyone his great news and there was no one to tell. Not only that, he was stuck with leftover meat loaf and doing the dumb laundry. Boy, some days you just couldn't win!

Just then the phone rang. It was his mom. His sister Kristin had had a baby boy and she and her husband, Mike, had decided to name the baby after Travis. Travis Alan Martin. Wow, that was really great! He had never had a baby named after him before.

By the time Travis was ready for bed, his mom was home and everything was pretty much back to normal. But Travis felt really tired. He had been turned inside out by everything that had happened to him that day. He felt as if he had been on a roller coaster the whole day and was just now getting off.

Lying in bed that night Travis thought about what Grandpa Joe always said about having to take the bad stuff of life along with the good stuff and not let the bad stuff blow you away. What was it he always said? "When life deals you a lemon, then make lemonade."

What had happened to Travis?

More to think about:

Which is more important? What happens *inside* us or what happens *outside* us? Why?

Have you ever felt like Travis?

How do you sort out what's really important and what's not so important?

It's Not Over Till It's Over

"So who are you going to vote for?" Steve asked his friends. All three boys stared hard at the three posters tacked on the wall next to the school cafeteria.

Evan shook his head. "No contest. Mike McGrath is going to beat out the other two guys without half-trying. He's the best quarterback in the NFL and everyone knows it's because of him we won the Super Bowl last year."

Larry nodded. "Yeah, maybe, but remember that we're voting for 'The Man of the Year' and Richie Right is the coolest dude around. He's got the greatest rock band our state has ever had and everyone knows that he and the Raging Rockets are going to go platinum again this year."

Steve shook his head. "You guys are forgetting about Frank Emerson. He was voted 'Teacher of the Year' last year and I know a lot of kids will be voting for him."

Evan pointed to the poster with Frank Emerson's picture on it and shook his head. "No way, man. It would take Mr. Emerson twenty zillion years to earn what Mike McGrath can earn in just one football game. We're talking major megabucks here."

47

Larry nodded again. "And Richie Right earns more with just one concert or one record than old man Emerson could earn in his whole life teaching at the junior high. Anyone with any brains knows that Richie Right is going to be named 'Man of the Year' for our state this year. His concerts are sold out all over the country and you can't even get a ticket unless you know someone who knows someone who knows someone."

Steve wrinkled up his nose and frowned. "I think I might just vote for Mr. Emerson. I think being a teacher is just as important as being a football hero or a rock star."

Larry rolled his eyes, "You're crazy, man. Mr. Emerson isn't going to get enough votes to fill a pop can. It's a two-man race. Richie Right and Mike McGrath."

Steve pointed to the picture of Richie Right. "Who's going to vote for a weirdo with green hair and purple paint all over his face? I bet he doesn't even know how to read a book."

Larry's face was becoming as red as his shirt. "Yeah, right. And like your Mr. Emerson is so perfect. I bet he can't even tell the difference between a football and a basketball. Who even knows Mr. Emerson? Maybe a few kids, but everyone in the whole state knows about Richie Right."

Now Steve's ears were beginning to turn red. "You're just a lot of hot air. Everyone in the whole state knows about Mr. Emerson. His picture was on the front page of the newspaper and he was even on the news last year."

Larry shrugged. "So big deal. Your Mr. Emerson was on the news one whole time last year. Richie Right is in the paper and on TV almost every week. Get real! You're voting for a loser and you're too dumb to even know it."

Evan let loose with a loud whistle. "Hey, guys, let's not get all heated up over this thing. Our votes don't count for anything anyway. It's not like we're going to really choose the 'Man of the Year,' you know."

Steve nodded. "I know our school is just voting for fun, but I still think we should take this thing seriously. And I still say that being a teacher is just as important as being some big sports hero or some big-head rock star."

Larry whacked Steve hard on the arm. "Just who are you calling a 'big-head rock star'? Your Mr. Emerson . . ."

Just then the bell rang and all the sixth graders lined up to cast their vote for the state's "Man of the Year" award.

Who do you think is going to win the real election? Why?

More to think about:

Who do you think will win the school election? Why?

Do you think Steve is really going to vote for Mr. Emerson? Why or why not?

Which do you think is more important: How much money a person earns or how much he helps other people?

How would you judge the value of a person?

Who would you vote for? Why?

What do you think voters should pay attention to when choosing a "Man of the Year"?

Judgment Call

Andrea jabbed Erica in the ribs. "See that boy over there by the water fountain? The one with the earring and the greasy hair? His name is Randall and I heard that he got kicked out of his old school and is here on probation to see if he can stay out of trouble."

Erica frowned. "What do you mean, 'stay out of trouble'? What did he do?"

Andrea leaned closer to Erica and whispered in her ear. "I heard that he was carrying a knife to school with a blade this long." Andrea held her hands apart to show how long the blade was.

"Did he ever use the knife on anyone?"

Andrea shook her head. "I don't think so. He told everyone he just wanted to have it on him in case he needed it. Yeah, right. Like if he needed it to cut someone up. Like maybe a teacher or someone who just looked at him the wrong way. So, anyway, I just wanted you to know that we're all going to steer clear of him. Maybe if everyone ignores him, he'll change schools again and take his problems somewhere else."

A boy in a blue football jersey waved to the two girls as he stuffed his jacket into his locker across from theirs and dug out a stack of books.

Andrea jabbed Erica again. "Now there's one cool dude. I just know Ryan's going to be class president again. He's just about the most popular guy in the whole school. Too bad that Randall kid isn't more like him."

At the pool that afternoon everyone was standing around waiting for class to start and Andrea was still talking about Ryan. Then the loud-speaker announced that Mr. Jordan wouldn't be there for class because of a family emergency, so class was canceled for the day.

Some of the guys on the other side of the pool let out a whoop and headed for the showers to change while three other guys started horsing around. Suddenly one of the guys slipped on the wet cement and ended up in the deep end of the pool shouting for help.

It was Toby. Toby was as wide as he was tall and he was waving his arms as he struggled to keep his head above water. The guys who had accidentally knocked him in the water dashed into the pool office to get help while some guy standing by the diving board dove into the water and headed straight for Toby.

The two girls watched as the boy pulled Toby to the edge of the pool. The kids on the side pulled Toby up out of the water and onto the cement, then pounded him on his back while he sputtered and coughed up water.

Andrea punched Erica on the arm. "I just know that was Ryan who jumped in like that. I've never seen anyone swim that fast ever. Let's go check it out."

The two girls raced around the far end of the pool and got there the same time as Coach Hardy.

Coach Hardy bent down to check on Toby, who was still coughing and sputtering but otherwise seemed to be okay.

The coach then stood up and slapped one of the guys on the shoulder. "Nice job, Randall. That was quick thinking on your part. You've got a powerful stroke there. You should try out for the swim team. I could use a guy like you. Be back here at 4:00 this afternoon and we'll see just what you can do."

Andrea opened her mouth, but nothing came out. Both girls just stood there staring at each other.

Why did Andrea think it was Ryan who had jumped in to save Toby?

More to think about:

Why is it important not to judge other people too quickly?

Do you think the kids will give Randall a chance? Why or why not?

How do you think Randall feels about having to change to a new school?

If you went to Randall's school, how would you treat him?

Do you think Randall will stay at his new school? Why or why not?

A Just Reward

Christmas was coming and everyone in Karen's family wanted to give her a special gift this year because she had worked so hard in school and helped so much around the house. She had even helped her younger sister, Sara, with her homework and her younger brother, Nick, build his rocket ship for the science fair.

Karen's dad decided to buy her the guitar she had been wanting for such a long time. He knew how much she loved music and he knew this would be a very special gift. He figured that Karen deserved the best, so he decided to go all out and buy her the most expensive guitar he could find.

Karen's mom decided to give her a gift certificate for a pair of designer jeans since all of Karen's friends wore designer jeans. Karen's family had never been able to afford to buy her the jeans, but this Christmas was special. Karen's mom figured that Karen deserved the best, so she bought a gift certificate which would allow Karen to buy the best of the best of designer jeans.

Karen's sister, Sara, wanted her gift for Karen to be special, too, so she decided that she would do all of Karen's household jobs for one whole week which would give Karen more time to spend with her friends. Sara knew that Karen especially hated cleaning the bathroom, so she put that at the top of the list of Karen's jobs she would do for the week.

Karen's brother, Nick, wanted his gift to be special also. He decided that he would use some of his allowance to buy her the new soccer ball he knew she wanted.

When he counted up his savings, he didn't have enough money to buy the soccer ball, so he found jobs in the neighborhood shoveling people's sidewalks and driveways to earn the extra money he needed.

Karen's grandmother was very impressed with all the gifts everyone was planning to give Karen and she thought for a very long time before deciding what to give Karen herself.

She didn't want to buy any guitars or designer jeans, but she wanted to give Karen a gift that would show her how much she loved her. She wasn't sure just what she could give Karen for Christmas that would be as special as all the other gifts.

After a lot of thinking, she finally decided to make Karen a certificate offering her ten hours of "talk time" to be used whenever and wherever Karen felt she just needed a good listener.

Everyone else in the family was so busy with all their activities that they were seldom home and Karen's grandmother figured she was almost always around doing something, baking her famous pastries, doing her needlework, or using the family computer. Besides, she had had a lot of practice listening to people for over fifty years and that was one thing she could do as well as anyone else—maybe better.

Everyone in the family ended up feeling very pleased with their gift selections and they could hardly wait for Christmas to come so they could make Karen happy.

Which gift do you think Karen will like the most? Why?

More to think about:

What do you think about Dad's gift?

What do you think about Mom's gift?

What do you think about Sara's gift?

What do you think about Nick's gift?

What do you think about the grandmother's gift?

Which gift would you have liked the most? Why?

A Long Way Home

Mr. Mansfield turned off the lights and turned on the projector. The kids in Jim's class quieted down and watched as the movie began.

The film was about two brothers. The older brother, Scott, had graduated from high school with honors and had gone on to college where he continued to do well. The younger brother, Martin, was nothing like Scott. Martin just managed to scrape by in high school and then joined a rock band instead of going on to college like his brother.

After graduating from college with honors, Scott returned home to help his father run the family business while Martin continued to roam all over the country with his rock band.

Scott continued to do well as usual. He was promoted from foreman to supervisor and then to manager.

Eventually Martin got tired of always being on the road and began to miss his family and the friends he had left back home. He was tired of playing his music in a different place every week and he was tired of the loud people. He had wanted to make the "big time," but this was certainly not his idea of the big time. Now he just wanted to go back home.

Martin finally decided to return home and ask his father for a job on the assembly line in his factory. He wasn't sure if his father would even accept him back home. Maybe he had forgotten all about him by now.

It took all the courage Martin had but he decided to go home. It took two days on the bus, and all that time he was wondering what his father would do when he saw him.

Would he tell him he was no longer welcome in his home? Would he tell him there was no work for him in his factory? Would he tell him to leave and never come back?

The bus finally pulled into the bus station in his hometown and Martin began the long hike out to the country where his family lived.

The sun was just going down as Martin finally got to the long winding road leading up to the house. Just as he reached the familiar mailbox, he saw his dad running down the road toward him with outstretched arms. Before Martin could say anything, his father hugged him and told him over and over again how much he had missed him and how glad he was that he had come home.

Martin's father gave him his old room back where nothing had been changed since he left. Even the old football and hockey pictures were still hanging on the wall. And the picture of Martin and his rock band was still on the desk where he had left it.

Once Martin was settled in, his father planned a huge welcome home party for him and Martin was treated like a king by everyone.

Scott was glad that his brother had finally come to his senses and returned home to do something constructive with his life, but he was also angry because of all the special treatment his brother was getting. It didn't seem fair that his brother, who had always made so many mistakes in his life, was now getting so much attention.

Scott wasn't so sure anymore that being the "good guy" really paid off; he was feeling more and more anger toward both his brother and his father.

The film ended with the father standing with his arms around both his sons with tears streaming down his face but looking very happy.

Mr. Mansfield shut off the projector and turned the lights back on and addressed the group. "So, gang, what do you think?"

Do you feel both sons were treated fairly by their father? Why or why not?

More to think about:

How do you feel about Scott?

How do you feel about Martin?

How do you feel about the father?

Do you think Martin will get a job in his father's factory?

If you were the father, how would you have treated Martin? Why?

Do you think Scott has a right to be angry at Martin and his father?

Making It Big

Leslie stared at the empty sheet of paper in front of her while she washed down another chocolate cookie with a glass of milk. She had to write an essay about the most successful person she knew and she didn't know where to begin.

As soon as Ms. Gleason announced the assignment in class, Leslie immediately knew who she would write her essay on. It had to be her Uncle Leonard.

Without a doubt, he was the biggest success she knew. He had dropped out of school in the ninth grade and made his own fortune in the lumber business. He and his wife now had a huge house with a swimming pool and a tennis court. They had two maids and even someone to drive their car. There was no doubt that he had made it big. And he had done it all on his own with no help from anyone else.

Her Uncle Leonard had everything he could ever want. He had expensive cars, he belonged to a country club, and he took fabulous vacations to new places Leslie had never even heard of. The only thing he didn't have was kids. But maybe he didn't want any kids because he was too busy doing all that fun stuff.

Then Leslie thought about her own family. There was her dad who taught at the local junior high. He would never make it big. He barely earned enough to keep food on the table and a roof over their heads. And the family hadn't taken a real vacation in years. They were lucky if they spent two weeks fishing at the lake up north all crowded together in a little cabin the size of her Uncle Leonard's garage.

Her father spent all his free time grading papers, helping his students with their problems, and coaching a Little League team. He never complained, but it sure wasn't much of a life. He never got to do any of the neat stuff Uncle Leonard did. Her dad didn't even own a set of golf clubs.

There were a lot of people who respected her dad and kids were always telling her how great her dad was, but what did he really have to show for all his hard work? Not much.

Then there was her mother who worked hard just taking care of a husband and five kids. Her mother always seemed to be working at cleaning house, cooking, or working with the learning disabled kids at the Learning Center.

Leslie was the youngest of the five kids and it was true that none of her brothers or sisters had any problems with drugs or alcohol and all five seemed to be turning out okay (at least so far), but what did her mother really have to show for all her hard work? Not much.

Leslie stopped chewing and picked up her pen. If she wrote the first sentence, the rest would probably just come to her, so she might as well begin.

"My Uncle Leonard is the most successful person I know. He has all the money anyone could ever want and he would never have to work another day in his whole life if he didn't want to."

Then she stopped writing and laid her pen down. She wondered why she kept thinking about her mom and dad when she had been all set to write her essay about her uncle.

Mom and Dad were nowhere near as successful as her uncle, so why was she still thinking about them?

Who do you think Leslie will write her essay about? Why?

More to think about:

Do you think Leslie's dad is happy? Why or why not?

Do you think Leslie's mom is happy? Why or why not?

What do you think it means to be a "success"?

Who is the most successful person you know?

What would you have to do to feel "successful"?

Moment of Truth

Mark took a deep breath as he watched the school bus come to a stop in front of him. He had dreaded this moment for over a month. The treatment for his drug problem had been no picnic, but returning to school was a thousand times worse. At least at the treatment center all the other kids had the same problem and no one was pointing fingers at him or whispering about him behind his back.

To make things a little easier his first day back, he had called his best friend, Lyle, last night and asked him to save him a seat on the school bus.

Mark straightened his shoulders and climbed onto the bus. Sure enough, there was Lyle, big as life, in the front seat, but he was sitting with Kevin and there was no room for Mark. Mark nodded to Lyle and headed to the back of the bus where there was still an empty seat.

Mark saw Lyle turn and look back at him once and then whisper something to Kevin. Kevin shrugged and whispered something to Lyle which made Lyle laugh.

By the time Mark got off the bus, Lyle and Kevin had already disappeared into the crowd of kids and it looked like Mark was on his own.

He took another deep breath and made his way to his locker. Some of the guys he usually hung out with were standing around Chad's locker laughing and joking.

Chad slugged Mark on the arm and greeted him like old times. "Glad you're back, buddy. We really missed you. Some of the guys are going bowling Friday night and then we're going to order in some pizza at my house afterward. I just want you to know that I fought like everything to get my parents to let you come, but they shot me down. Maybe next time."

Mark nodded. "Yeah, maybe next time." He slammed his locker door shut and headed for the science lab. On the way to the lab, he passed several kids he knew, but no one said anything. It was like they didn't even see him.

By the time Mark got to the lab, Mr. Webster was already assigning lab partners.

Mr. Webster shot him a big smile. "Welcome back, Mark. Okay, class, Mark is going to need a lab partner. Who has room for Mark in their group for today's experiment?"

No one raised their hand. His usual partner, Reuben, just stared down at his book but didn't say anything. Mark heard a few snickers, but no one raised their hand.

Somewhere from the back of the room, someone said, "I already have a lab partner, but Mark can join Kurt and me if he wants to."

It was Justin, the class brain. Mark had done his share of poking fun at Justin himself. The red hair, the thick glasses, and the braces on his teeth. Not exactly the kind of kid you wanted to pal around with.

And Kurt wasn't much better. He always had his head stuck in a book and he couldn't drop a basket in gym class even if he was standing right next to the net with no one guarding him.

The day was quickly going from bad to disastrous and Mark could feel his cheeks flashing neon red as he dropped his books down on the lab table next to Justin and Kurt and Mr. Webster began explaining the experiment.

While Mr. Webster talked about reptiles, mammals, and amphibians, Mark thought about betrayal, deceit, and humiliation. The whole day had been like something from *The Twilight Zone* and there was no reason to think tomorrow would be any better.

What do you think Mark is going to do about his problem?

More to think about:

What do you think about how Lyle behaved on the bus?

What do you think about how Reuben reacted in class?

If Mark had been your friend, what would you have done?

Do you think Mark will begin using drugs again? Why or why not?

What would you do if you had Mark's problem?

"MVP"

Coach Taylor called his team over to the dugout. He pulled his cap off his head and wiped his forehead with his sleeve. "Okay, guys, listen up. We've got a big problem here.

"Todd has wrenched his shoulder and can't pitch today, which means that Ricky or Ken will have to pitch. We can cover all the bases if Sam takes Ricky's place on first and Tim takes Ken's place on third.

"But I also need to move Joe out of left field up to shortstop, so that leaves a spot in left field we've got to cover just for today and then tomorrow everyone can go back to playing their regular positions."

Coach Taylor looked hard at both Ricky and Ken. "One of you guys will have to pitch and one of you will have to play left field if we're going to get through this game the best way we can. I know this is going to be a tough decision for both of you, but this team is all about 'teamwork' and I need you to do what's best for the team."

Ken shook his head, moving a huge wad of gum around inside his cheek. "Thanks, but no thanks, coach. My dad is going to be here today to watch me play and he'll never even see me if I'm stuck out in left field. No one ever bangs anything out there and I'm not about to stand around counting butterflies and dandelions. Sorry, Coach, but count me out."

Ricky stood in the corner of the dugout, making circles in the dirt with his shoe, just listening. He dug his hands deeper into his pockets and stared at the pitcher's mound. His whole family was coming to the game as usual, but his grandparents were also coming to see him play before they returned home to Arizona. They had never seen him play and they had been talking about it all week. Boy, would they be impressed if they could see him pitch. They would be so proud they'd probably be telling everyone back home in Sun City about it for the next year.

Then he stared out into left field. Ken was right. There was never any action out there. He might as well be sitting in the stands as standing out there. No one on the team really wanted to play left field. The guys even had a name for it. The "nowhere position."

But Ricky also knew that Coach Taylor was in a tight spot and had to use his players the best way he could for the good of the whole team. The Panthers were a tough team and Ricky's team, the Lions, were already considered the underdog for today's game. The Lions needed all the help they could get.

Ricky could feel the sweat rolling down the back of his neck and his mouth felt like it was stuffed with the whole jar of his mom's cotton balls. He didn't want to do it, but he knew what he had to do.

"I can play left field and Ken can pitch today," Ricky finally said, grabbing a fielder's mitt from the stack of equipment and not looking at any of the other guys.

Coach Taylor wiped his forehead again and pulled his cap back on. "Thanks, Ricky, I owe you one. This is going to be a tough game today and we need everyone looking sharp. Okay, guys, let's get out there and give it our best shot and remember, 'All for one and one for all!' "

The boys all gave the coach a high-five and headed to their assigned positions. Ken flashed Ricky a thumbs-up sign and headed to the pitcher's mound with a big grin while Ricky slipped on his glove and headed out to left field.

Who do you think the team will give the "Most Valuable Player" award to after today's game? Why?

More to think about:

Who do you think should get the "MVP" award?

If you were Ricky, what would you have done?

How do you think Ricky's family will feel when they find out what he has done?

Can you think of any other way Coach Taylor could have worked out the team's problem?

What does it mean to be a "team player"?

No Rules

Phil and Brian had been best friends since first grade. Now they were in the sixth grade and they were still best friends, at least until this year. Now they had a really big problem—their dads.

Phil's dad let him do just about anything he wanted to do. Phil had no curfew and could stay out as late as he wanted. His dad just told him to stay out of trouble and "keep his nose clean." Phil didn't even have to be home for meals. He could eat whatever and whenever he wanted and his dad didn't even complain when he pigged out on junk food.

Last week Phil failed two math tests and all his dad said was that "math was getting harder all the time." His dad didn't say anything about Phil studying harder and Phil didn't lose any of his TV privileges.

Then there was Brian's dad. Brian not only had a very strict curfew, but he could get grounded for a whole week if he was late by even a few minutes. Phil had never been grounded for anything in his entire life.

And as far as meals, not only did Brian have to be home on time for meals, he had to help with the dishes afterward. And sometimes he even had to help with the cooking if his mother was going to be late. There was no junk food anywhere in the house, so Brian always got stuck eating the healthy stuff.

And then there was his homework. Brian couldn't watch any TV at all until his homework was done. And if he ever failed a test, he knew he probably wouldn't be watching any more TV for the rest of his life.

Brian also missed out on a lot of the parties that Phil got to go to. If the parents of the kid giving the party weren't going to be there during the whole party, then Brian wasn't allowed to go. There were even times when Brian's dad had actually called the family of the friend giving the party to be sure they were going to be there.

And then there was the phone. Phil had his own phone line and could talk whenever he wanted for as long as he wanted, while Brian had a fifteen-minute limit on all his phone calls. Brian's dad told both Brian and his sister that fifteen minutes was the limit, so that they didn't tie up the line for the rest of the family.

There were times Brian wished his dad was really cool like Phil's dad.

Phil's dad felt Phil would learn more by making his own mistakes, so he set no limits for Phil at all. He always told Phil that if he got into trouble, it was up to Phil to get himself out of trouble, so he better think before he did anything dumb.

Brian's dad believed he had a responsibility as a parent to give Brian guidance and to help keep him from making too many unnecessary mistakes. He had a saying that a foolish man didn't learn from his own mistakes, a smart man did learn from his own mistakes, and a wise man learned from the mistakes of others.

Brian's dad told him that he knew Brian would have to make some mistakes because that was just part of growing up, but he hoped that Brian could also learn from others' mistakes as well.

If you had to decide which boy is happier, who would it be: Phil or Brian?

More to think about:

What do you think of Phil's dad?

Do you think Phil is lucky to have a dad like that? Why or why not?

Do you think Phil ever feels scared having so much freedom? Why or why not?

What do you think of Brian's dad?

Which dad would you rather have? Why?

Not Fair

The bell rang and all the kids ran out the door. Everyone except Kim.

Kim remained at her desk staring at the math paper in front of her, a big red "F" staring back at her.

She slammed her notebook shut so hard that Mr. Jackson stopped correcting papers and looked up.

He smiled and put down his pen. "It sounds like I've got an unhappy customer here."

Kim wiped away a tear that was making its way down her cheek. "Mr. Jackson, I just can't keep up with the class. I have to babysit my little sister every day after school till my mom gets home. Then I have to help with dinner and dishes. And then I have to feed my hamsters. I just have too much to do right now to do all my homework."

Mr. Jackson came over and sat down on the corner of Kim's desk. "It sounds like you're feeling pretty overworked right now. Would you like me to work with you during your free period till you catch on to percentages?"

Kim shook her head. "I don't think that would help. I understand every-thing you tell us in class, but then when I'm on my own, everything just seems to fly out of my head and I don't remember anything. I need a quiet place to study, but I have to share my bedroom with my little sister so I don't have any quiet place at home where I can really work hard."

"Have you tried talking to your parents and telling them how you feel?"

Kim shrugged and shook her head. "I don't want to bug them with my problems. They have enough problems of their own just starting their new business and everything."

Mr. Jackson thought a moment. "Do you think talking to Ms. Dean, the guidance counselor, would help? Would you like me to make an appointment for you to see her?"

Kim shook her head again. "No, I don't think I need to talk to her. I just have too much on my mind right now to really pay attention to my math, or anything else for that matter. I'm falling behind in my science class, too."

Mr. Jackson nodded to Dennis in the hallway as he rolled by in his wheelchair, his lap loaded with books and his tape player. Dennis smiled back and gave him a thumbs-up sign.

Kim folded her math paper and stuck it in her math book. "I just don't know what I'm going to do. I love my sister, but I'm beginning to feel more like her mother than her sister. Sometimes I even wish I didn't have a sister."

As Mr. Jackson helped Kim load up her books, Emily stopped by to tell Mr. Jackson that she had signed up for Ms. Dean's "Kids of Divorce" group and that her mother had joined a group to help her with her drinking problem, so things were going a little better at home. Emily said it even looked like her younger brother might be moving back home soon from his foster home.

Mr. Jackson gave Emily a high-five and then helped Kim strap on her backpack. "Kim, I'll make a deal with you. If you can find one other kid at this school who doesn't have any problems, I'll wipe out that F and let you take the test over again."

Kim let loose with the beginning of a smile. "You've got to be kidding. I just have to find one kid in this whole school who doesn't have a problem? Piece of cake, Mr. Jackson! You've got yourself a deal. Thanks a lot."

Do you think Kim will be able to find someone with no problems? Why or why not?

More to think about:

If you were Kim, what would you do about her problems?

Do you think Dennis has problems?

What about Emily and her problems?

Do you think everyone has problems?

What's your most difficult problem right now and what are you doing about it?

Number One

Nick and Tony had looked forward all year to the final track meet of the season and they were more than ready for it. They had already won more ribbons than anyone else at the smaller meets and they were sure to do well in the finals. It was just a matter of which one of them came in first and which one came in second in the different events.

The day of the meet finally arrived and both boys started off on their bikes. They were in high spirits thinking about all the events they were going to enter and all the ribbons they were going to win. Since this was the biggest track meet of the year, a trophy was going to be awarded to the highest point earner for the day and both Nick and Tony knew that one of them was sure to win the trophy.

The season track trophy was two feet tall and whoever won it would get his picture in the school paper and probably in the city newspaper, the *Metro Daily*, as well. Whoever won that trophy would for sure be *Number One!*

Just as Nick and Tony approached the turnoff to the track meet, Nick heard a soft whimpering coming from the brush next to the road. He laid his bike down in the grass and walked back slowly looking for whatever was making the sound.

Tony was already up the road and called back to Nick to hurry up. This was one track meet they didn't want to be late for. Nick waved Tony to go on ahead and yelled back that he'd catch up with him as soon as he could.

It didn't take long for Nick to find the problem. There in the tall grass next to the road was a black puppy. It couldn't be more than four or five months old and it was all curled up in a ball licking its side.

By the time Nick found the puppy, Tony was back to see what was taking Nick so long. Both boys examined the puppy and agreed that it must have been hit by a car and tossed up into the tall grass. Maybe the driver never even knew he hit him.

Nick couldn't tell how hurt the dog was, but it was clear it couldn't get anywhere on its own and needed help right away.

Nick gently wrapped the puppy in his extra track shirt and then carefully loaded him into his backpack. Then he slowly put his backpack on and climbed onto his bike.

Nick told Tony to go ahead to the track meet while he got the puppy to the vet in town. Tony couldn't believe his ears. Nick was crazy to take a stray dog to the vet and miss the race.

He reminded Nick that the vet was more than five miles away and by the time Nick got back to the meet, it would be half over and he'd have no chance at all to win the trophy. Besides that, he'd probably be too tired to even win any ribbons.

Tony told Nick to put the dog by the side of the road where he could be seen and let someone else take care of him. Tony was sorry the dog was hurt, but it wasn't his problem or Nick's. Besides, maybe the vet would make Nick pay for taking care of the dog. It could be fifty bucks or more. Better to leave the dog by the side of the road and let someone else help him. Someone would be sure to see him and get him the help he needed.

But Nick shook his head and told Tony to go on to the track meet without him and that he would get back as soon as he could.

So Nick took off for the vet and Tony headed on to the meet, sure to win first place in just about every event and a sure bet to win the trophy now that Nick wouldn't be there.

Which boy do you think was the real winner that day? Why?

More to think about:

Why do you think Tony went on to the track meet?

Why do you think Nick stayed with the dog?

Do you think Nick will someday wish he hadn't helped the dog and missed all or part of the track meet? Why or why not?

How do you think Nick will feel if Tony wins the trophy?

What would you have done if you had been there? Why?

One Wish

Ms. Murphy opened a book and called the class to attention. "Okay, class, today we're going to read a story about two sisters and a magic fairy."

Some groans came from the back of the room, but Ms. Murphy ignored them and began reading. "Once many years ago in a land not so very far away, there were two sisters who had a very magical experience. They were just two very ordinary girls living a very ordinary life until one day a magic fairy appeared to them and granted each sister one wish. She told them they could have anything they wanted, anything at all.

"The first sister needed no time to think, she knew just what she would wish for. She wished for an easy life with no problems and all the money she would ever need so that she would never have to work a day in her life.

"The second sister thought for a long time and then finally she wished for a happy heart. She wished that whatever happened to her, she would be able to try hard and always have a good outlook on life.

"As the years went by, the first sister did get everything she could ever want. A huge house with many servants, a fancy car, designer clothes, expensive jewelry, and friends who shared her jet-set life.

"The second sister had to work for everything she got. She made it through college by earning scholarships and by working long hours in the school cafeteria. Then after college she went on to law school and spent most of her evenings studying in the library instead of going to parties with her friends.

"After she passed her bar exam, she was offered a job with a private law firm where she could earn a ton of money and work with some very famous people. She seriously considered the offer, but finally decided that that really wasn't what she wanted to do.

"Instead, she joined a small law practice in a very poor section of town with rundown buildings and a high crime rate. But through all these trials, she did have a happy heart."

Ms. Murphy closed the book and smiled. "Okay, class, if we roll this story ahead ten years, which sister do you think is going to be the happier? The sister who was given everything on a silver platter and never had to work a day in her life or the sister who had to earn everything by her own efforts? I don't want you to answer now. I want you to think about this story and we'll talk about it some more tomorrow."

All the way home Johanna thought about the story. She imagined herself as the sister with the huge house and all the servants. Wow, that would be really great. Nothing to worry about. Who could ask for anything more than that? That sister had to be the happier one.

Then she thought about the other sister. All she did was work, work,

work. And even after working her way through college and law school, she didn't even end up with a decent job. It sounded like she'd be working hard the rest of her life. What a bummer!

Then Johanna thought about her friend Melissa. Melissa never had to ask for anything. She got stuff before she even asked for it. Like that great tent and the playhouse next to the swimming pool. And how about all the karate and gymnastics lessons her dad paid for? Melissa didn't even seem to appreciate half the stuff she had.

Then Johanna thought about her own karate uniform she had to earn by raking leaves. And when she had wanted that antique doll, she had to earn half the money for it by helping clean out the garage. Working for that karate uniform had made it very special and the doll she had to help pay for was her favorite one.

Who do you think Johanna will decide is the happier of the two sisters? Why?

More to think about:

Which sister do you think was the happier sister? Why?

How do you feel when you get something for nothing?

How do you feel when you earn what you get?

Is working hard for something good or bad? Why?

If someone offered to make your one wish come true, what would your one wish be? Why?

Three Strikes

Courtney had been looking forward to her birthday party for more than a month. She had invited her three best friends for a Friday night sleepover and now she was busy planning everything.

She was seriously trying to decide between sausage, hamburger, and pepperoni pizza when the phone rang. It was Jennifer calling to let her know that she wouldn't be able to come to the overnight after all because a special skiing trip had just come up which was "just too terrific to turn down."

Somehow Courtney wasn't all that surprised. This wasn't the first time Jennifer had dropped out at the last minute. She had been all excited about going to the circus with Courtney and her family last spring until a friend invited her to go camping. And then that was that. Jennifer went camping. And then there was last week when Jennifer was going to go to the karate tournament with Courtney. Then Jennifer got invited to Tara's surprise birthday party. Jennifer forgot all about the karate tournament and went to the party.

Even though Courtney knew she couldn't really count on Jennifer, she still felt disappointed. Jennifer was a lot of fun and Courtney liked hanging out with her.

Courtney knew she could always count on Beth, so she reached for the phone. Talking over her party plans with Beth would help her feel better.

But as soon as Courtney mentioned the party Friday night, Beth suddenly got quiet. There was a long pause and then Beth gave Courtney the bad news.

Beth had to cancel out too because her dad had just given her two tickets to a rock concert for Friday night which was an "absolute once-in-a-lifetime" opportunity.

Beth said she would have invited Courtney to go with her, but she knew that Courtney was having the overnight and couldn't go, so Beth invited her cousin to go with her instead.

By now Courtney was feeling more than just a little down, she was feeling *really* down. But she knew she could always count on Stephanie to cheer her up, so she reached for the phone again.

Unfortunately, Stephanie only had more bad news for her. She couldn't come to the overnight either because her brother's basketball team had made it to the playoffs and their big game was Friday night. Stephanie offered to come over to Courtney's after the game, but there was no way of knowing how late that would be.

By now Courtney was feeling about as down as she had ever felt in her whole life, like she had hit rock bottom, when Carol called to ask about a homework assignment.

Carol was not very popular at Courtney's school because she was so shy and kept pretty much to herself. She seemed to spend most of her time by herself with her head buried in a book. She even brought her own lunch every day and ate it by herself in the school library instead of eating in the cafeteria with the rest of the kids.

Carol was not the kind of kid you wanted to pal around with. She was the one you might do homework with, but you wouldn't invite her to a pizza party or to go roller skating. Or to an overnight.

But why not? On the spur of the moment, Courtney asked Carol if she'd like to do something with her Friday night to help her celebrate her birthday. Then Courtney waited, half expecting Carol to say no.

But Carol immediately accepted the invitation and both girls excitedly began to make their plans.

Which of the four girls would you want for a friend? Why?

More to think about:

What do you think of Jennifer? Would you want her for a friend? Why or why not?

What about Beth?

What about Stephanie?

What is a real friend?

Are you a real friend to someone?

Three-Way Split

"Wow, Laura, look at these. These earrings have my own birthstone and there's only one pair left. I've always wanted earrings just like this."

Laura stopped to look at the earrings Tess was so excited about. "They're really pretty, but we're here to finish our Christmas shopping and we've already lost Melanie. I'll go try to find her while you finish up and we'll meet you at the checkout counters."

A few minutes later Laura returned with Melanie, their carts loaded with Christmas gifts. As they headed for the checkout counter with the shortest line, they spotted Tess still at the earring counter.

They headed over toward her and then stopped dead in their tracks. They watched Tess bend over and slip the earrings into her boot and then continue looking at the earring cards on the rack. Laura couldn't believe her eyes. She was sure Tess had never shoplifted anything before, but that's exactly what she was doing now.

Laura and Melanie just stood there for a minute staring at Tess, not sure what to do. Then Melanie told Laura she was going to pay for her purchases and she'd meet them outside.

Laura grabbed the handle of Melanie's cart and held onto it. She told her that they couldn't just let their best friend do something that could get her into a lot of trouble. They had to do something to help her and fast.

Melanie shook her head and told Laura that what Tess did was her business. If Tess wanted to do something dumb, that was her choice, but there was nothing they could do about it. They weren't her mother. Besides, real friends accepted each other just as they are without trying to change them. Nobody was perfect and it wasn't up to either of them to tell Tess what to do or what not to do.

As Melanie headed in the other direction toward one of the registers with her cart, Laura headed over to Tess. She just couldn't agree with Melanie. She wasn't about to stand by and do nothing while her best friend made a stupid mistake for a silly pair of earrings she didn't even need.

As Tess started to push her shopping cart toward the nearest register, Laura stopped her and told her to put the earrings back before she ended up in real trouble.

Tess gave Laura a dirty look and told her she didn't know what she was talking about. She also told her to mind her own business and then started checking out her purchases.

Laura got in line behind Tess and held her breath while Tess paid for all the Christmas gifts in her cart. So far, so good. No bells or buzzers went off and no huge security guard grabbed Tess and demanded to search her.

Tess headed for the exit with her bags while Laura breathed a sigh of relief and paid for her own purchases.

When Laura caught up with Melanie and Tess outside the store, they were almost doubled over with laughter. Tess was showing Melanie the earrings and telling her how easy it had been. No one had suspected anything.

Melanie told Tess how "totally awesome" the whole thing was and how she would never have been able to pull off anything like that. Her face would have turned bright red, her hands would have been shaking like crazy, and she would have fallen apart before she even got to the door. Just wait till the kids at school heard what Tess had done. They just wouldn't believe it.

As the three girls headed for the hamburger shop next door, Laura began to unwind and relax a little, but she wondered if her friendship with Tess and Melanie would ever really be the same after this.

Who do you think was the better friend to Tess—Melanie or Laura? Why?

More to think about:

What do you think about what Tess did?

What do you think about Melanie's way of handling the situation?

What do you think about Laura's concern?

If you had been there, what would you have done? Why?

Do you think the girls' friendship will ever be the same again? Why or why not?

Too Far Away

Mr. Mansfield shut off the projector and turned the lights back on. "So that's what a famine looks like. Up close. With real people with real names. What did you think of the film?"

Matt raised his hand. "I thought the film was really sad. All those little kids with big bellies and skinny arms and legs. And all those flies around the babies who were too weak to move. But Africa is pretty far away and what can our class do about such a big problem? There's only thirty of us and there's thousands of starving kids over there. Maybe more. We wouldn't even make a dent in a problem that big, no matter what we did."

Jodi's hand shot up. "Matt has a point, but I don't think I agree with everything he said. I think we *can* make a difference even if we just help one starving child. What if that one child were your brother or your sister? Wouldn't you feel it was worth it? I remember a story my grandfather told me about a little boy who was walking along a beach throwing starfish back into the ocean. An old man asked him what difference he could possibly make when there were so many starfish and he couldn't throw all of them back into the ocean. The boy just picked up one starfish and said to the old man, 'It makes a big difference to this one.' Then the boy just kept on walking and throwing the starfish back into the ocean. I always thought it would make a great ending to the story if the old man started throwing the starfish back into the ocean too, but I guess he didn't."

Before Mr. Mansfield could say anything, Matt raised his hand again. "I'm just saying that I think we should be very careful where we put our money since we don't have all that much in the first place. Whatever money we earn from our car wash and our spaghetti supper should go to some project where we can really make a difference. Like that family on the news last night. They lost their home and everything in it in the fire and they don't even have a place to sleep. And the kids don't have any clothes or toys or anything. I say we should help someone who's a lot closer than Africa."

Tracy's hand was the next to go up. "But what if everyone felt that way? Then no one would contribute anything to the really big problems and those problems would just get bigger."

Shannon shook her head. "I think I've got to agree with Matt. We're just one small group. Let the large charities take care of the big problems and let us take care of something we can really handle. Like that family Matt is talking about."

Jeremy wrinkled up his forehead and pushed his glasses back up on his nose. "I hear what everyone is saying, but I don't think it makes much difference whether the problem is large or small. I think we can still make a difference if we choose to tackle one small part of even a really big problem. What if we use our money to buy two oxen to help the people farm their land in Rwanda or what if we choose to sponsor one child through one of the large charities. Then we know we are making a difference even though the problem is a very large one."

Mr. Mansfield looked thoughtful. "I think you have all contributed some very valuable thoughts on this question and I will leave it up to the group to decide where you want to put your money. Think about it, talk it over, and we'll do more planning next time. I might just add that I believe any effort to help people is a good use of your money, so you're all on the right track. See you next time."

If you were in Matt's group, how would you feel about the discussion?

More to think about:

Who is your "neighbor"? Only the people in your neighborhood? What about people in another country or even across the world?

Do you really believe you can make a difference if the problem is very big? Why or why not?

How do you feel after you help someone?

How do you feel after someone helps you?

If you were in Matt's group, who would receive your money? Why?

Tough Sweat

Paula closed her eyes and counted to ten, hoping somehow things would look better when she opened them. But they didn't. All she could do was stare blankly at what was left of her Tyrannosaurus Rex. Yesterday the dinosaur skeleton had been almost four feet tall and looking great. Today, his bones were all jumbled up on the floor and he was definitely not looking good.

It had taken her almost two weeks to put the dinosaur skeleton together from the model kit her dad had given her for her birthday. It was two weeks for nothing. Now all she had left was a pile of bones.

Paula glared at her dog, Patches, lying with his head on his paws watching her. The dog was looking very guilty. Well, he *should* look guilty. He had destroyed in minutes what it had taken her two weeks to put together. Either it was the smell of the glue that had lured Patches to do what he did, or he was just feeling bored and had nothing better to do.

The school science fair was only a week away and there was no way Paula could rebuild the skeleton in seven days unless she spent every waking moment working on it. And she wasn't about to do that.

Forget the science fair! She had better things to do with her time, like playing video games at the arcade or going bowling with her friends.

Her model weather station had won second prize last year and her science teacher, Mr. Webster, told her she had a good chance of winning first prize this year. Science was her favorite class and the science projects and lab experiments the other kids hated, she really had fun doing.

Putting together the dinosaur again would be fun in a way now that she knew how to do it. But not if she had to race against the clock. Should she try to put her dinosaur model back together in time for the science fair or just forget the whole thing?

She knew what her dad would say. He loved a challenge. The bigger the challenge, the more excited he got and the harder he worked—like the doll house he built for Paula when she was eight. She wanted to give up when the roof somehow ended up not fitting quite right on top of the house, but her dad never for a minute considered giving up. He just kept working on it till he got it right. For sure, he would tell her to go for it.

And Grandmother Bessie? She had been so proud of Paula last year when her weather station came in second at the fair. Paula knew that her grandmother would want her to hang in there and try for first place this year.

But Paula told herself that *she* was the one who would be stuck gluing a zillion dinosaur bones back together again. Not her dad and not her grandmother. This was her decision, not theirs.

She knew what her friends would tell her. They already thought she was a dork for spending so much time building her T. Rex in the first place. They'd think she was totally bonkers if she dropped out of sight for a whole week just to rebuild the same dumb old dinosaur all over again.

Her friends were right. Why should she spend a whole week of her life sweating bullets while they were out having fun without her?

What do you think Paula will do? Why?

More to think about:

If you were Paula, what would you do? Why?

What do you think Mr. Webster, the science teacher, would want Paula to do?

How do you think Paula will feel if she doesn't enter the science fair this year?

How do you think Paula will feel if she tries to put her T. Rex back together again?

Which do you think is more important? Winning an award at the science fair or finishing a project the way you think it should be done? Why?

Where Did Everybody Go?

If there was one thing Jeff avoided, it was work. When it was time to help his mother make dinner, he always managed to be outside playing baseball with his friends or out in the garage working on his model planes. Anywhere far enough away, so he didn't get stuck setting the table or cutting up carrots for Mom.

And when it was time to help his brother with the dishes after dinner, he always managed to disappear upstairs to his room to work on his stamp collection. He always turned up the volume on his stereo so loud that he couldn't hear his brother if he did call him.

When his dad asked him to help clean out the garage, Jeff was always ready with a good excuse. There was a big test he had to study for or homework that would take him hours to finish. He was always ready with a good excuse for any situation.

It was no different at school. When someone had to clean the blackboards, he never volunteered. When the class needed to make posters for the rummage sale, he said he was too busy. And when the principal, Mr. Stewart, asked for volunteers to pick up litter on the school grounds after school, he never raised his hand.

Jeff had learned to avoid just about every job that came his way. He knew that if he didn't do it, someone else always would. So why should he worry about it? Let someone else do the "jerk work" while he did the stuff he enjoyed.

Toward the end of March, it was his turn for his beaver pack to meet at his house. The April meeting was always the most important meeting because the guys would be planning their summer camping trip, which was always a lot of fun. The camping trip was the big event of the whole year and Jeff even had his own canoe.

Jeff wanted everything to be just perfect for the meeting, so he asked his mother if she would bake some cookies for the group. She told him she would love to, but she was going to be busy going places with her friends all week and just wouldn't have time to do any extra baking.

Jeff asked his brother if he could help him get his ecology project finished for the meeting. His brother told him he would be glad to help, but he just didn't have any extra time because he was so busy taking care of all his regular jobs around the house.

Then Jeff asked his dad if he could pick up two of the guys who didn't have rides for the meeting. His dad told him he would like to do that, but he just was too busy still working on the garage to be able to do it. Maybe next time.

It looked like it was going to be up to Jeff to do everything for the meeting. But he couldn't do everything all by himself, so he asked two of his friends from his class who were in his beaver pack to help him out.

Rob told Jeff he was sorry but he couldn't help because he would be busy picking up litter on the school grounds until the meeting, and Gene told him that he couldn't help out because he would be busy making posters for the rummage sale until the meeting.

Jeff was getting madder by the minute. Why wasn't anyone willing to help him when he really needed help? It just wasn't fair that he had to do everything by himself. Where were people when you really needed them anyway?

Do you think Jeff will find someone to help him? Why or why not?

More to think about:

Why is no one willing to help Jeff?

Do you think Jeff will figure out why no one is willing to help him?

Do you know someone like Jeff?

Are you sometimes like Jeff?

If you were Jeff, what would you do?

Who's in the Kitchen?

Mrs. Saunders came home from work Thursday afternoon totally wiped out. She stretched out on the couch and called both of her daughters in to see if one of them would make dinner while she relaxed for a while in a nice warm bath.

Lori told her mother that she would be glad to make dinner, but she had already promised her friend Jill that she would be right over to help her study for the big math test tomorrow. Maybe she could make dinner Friday night instead.

Robin had no special plans for the night so she told her mother to go enjoy a long soak in the tub and she would be glad to make dinner and even do the dishes.

Mrs. Saunders went off to relax in a warm bath feeling much better already. It was great knowing that she no longer had to worry about making dinner or doing dishes. It looked like it was going to be an okay night after all.

It was wonderful having a daughter like Robin who was willing to help out when things got a little tough. How many kids would be so willing to help out and even offer to do more than was asked of them? Probably not too many. She would have to do something special for Robin to let her know how much she appreciated her help.

Robin knew she had plenty of time to make dinner, so she went off to her room to listen to her new rap tapes for a while before starting dinner.

Since she had so much time, she also decided to call her friend Trisha, so they could begin making their plans for the weekend. Maybe they could begin working on their Halloween costumes so they'd be ready for the party at school next week.

When Robin called Trisha, she found out that Trisha was thinking about having a Halloween party at her house instead of going trick-or-treating this year. That was great news and Robin and Trisha began making plans for the party. Robin intended to help her mother by making dinner but somehow she lost track of time. There were so many decisions to make for the party. Which kids to invite, what games to play, and what food to have? And, of course, what costumes to wear.

Lori was already out the door and on her way to Jill's when she began to feel a little guilty about not helping her mother. Especially since her mother had been working two jobs since the divorce last year.

She knew Jill was depending on her to help her study for her math test, but her mother also needed some help right now, too. Maybe she could figure out a way to help both of them.

Lori headed back home and called Jill to let her know that she'd be over at six instead of five to help her study for the math test. She told Jill to go over last week's math test so that she would know what things she needed to practice. Then Lori went off to the kitchen to help Robin with dinner, feeling a lot better.

An hour later Mrs. Saunders was feeling more like her old self after her bath and headed toward the kitchen to see how dinner was coming along. She could smell something really good, something with a lot of onion and garlic.

As she passed Robin's room, she found her still stretched out on her bed listening to tapes and talking on the phone.

So then who was in the kitchen? Mrs. Saunders made her way through all the living room clutter to the kitchen where she found Lori busy setting the table while she kept an eye on the spaghetti sauce simmering on the stove.

Who do you think was the more responsible daughter? Robin or Lori? Why?

More to think about:

What do you think about Robin? Were her intentions good?

What do you think about Lori? Why did she change her mind about helping her mother?

Is it enough to have good intentions if you don't follow through and do what you said you would do?

If you tell someone you're going to do something, how important is it that you do it?

Have you ever promised to do something and then not done it? How did you feel?